"I Can't Come To School Today... My Mom's In Prison And I Don't Have A Ride."

Kathleen Van Antwerp

"I Can't Come To School Today... My Mom's In Prison And I Don't Have A Ride."

Kathleen Van Antwerp

Quiet Thunder
PUBLISHING

"I Can't Come To School Today...
My Mom's In Prison And I Don't Have A Ride."

A Collection of Stories
Kathleen Van Antwerp

Published by:

Quiet Thunder Publishing
P.O. Box 2097
Ventura, CA 93002

Cover design by Liliana McAndrew

Printed in the U.S.A.

Library of Congress Catalog Card Number: 97-68836
ISBN 0-9659143-9-9

Publisher's Cataloging-in-Publication
(Provided by Quality Books, Inc.)

Van Antwerp, Kathleen.
       I can't come to school today--My Mom's in prison and I don't
    have a ride : a collection of stories / Kathleen Van Antwerp. --
    1st ed.
       p. cm.
       ISBN: 0-9659143-9-9
       1. Abused children--Education--Case studies. 2. Sexually abused
    teenagers--Education--Case studies. 3. Socially handicapped
    teenagers--Education--Case studies. 4. Special education. I.
    Title.

    LC4085.V36 1997   371.9
                                                    QBI97-40842

Dedication

We floated out to
sea—
We sat under the
stars —
It was there that these
stories
came to life —
because you listened
to me.

Acknowledgements

"You Can Keep My Thank You Forever" he said.

He was four years old and didn't have a family. He did have gratitude and he gave it to me. It was the best lesson and one of the kindest gifts I'd ever received.

...So to all of you who have believed in this book and the words of these children.

"I give you my thank you, and please...you can keep my thank you forever."

For the ever-present love and support from my parents and family–thank you.

Dr. Carol Kelly–may the child mental health specialist program continue to advocate and educate on behalf of children. Thank you for the foundation you've given me.

This is the rare moment when I thank my brother, Steve, for correcting my English.

Liliana–thank you for sharing your talent. This is one book I hope people judge by its cover!

With every word you typed, you believed. Thank you for coming along on this journey, Rose Navarro.

From one writer to another, I appreciate and respect your opinions, Beth. Thank you.

Dr. Sue Sears, Dr. Richard Mesaros, Sandy Enfield, Sharon Van Velzer, Daniel Little, Phillip Gore, Jeanne Dukes, Laura Huebner, Terry & Ron Weed, Pamela Fernandez, Christine Donaldson, Linda Glover, Tracey Grevatt.

Our dreams have taken on meaning–I understand why doves mate for life...thank you Dorn. I love you.

Contents

Introduction

I don't know if I'm a writer, but I know these stories need to be told. That thought is exactly how this book was born, through stories being told.

I shared the stories of these beautiful children who have touched my life and those whose ears received these stories encouraged me to share with others.

Those of you who read this book are the others who will be touched by these children. Their lives are the lives nobody wants to live.

As you read this book, let them into your mind, your heart and your soul. By doing so, you give them life and they, in some small way, become somebody's children.

The following collection of stories describes
at-risk children, includes excerpts from
their writing and demonstrates classroom
techniques that helped me reach them.
The italicized portion of each story was left in
its original form as written by each child.
All names have been changed to protect the
identity of these individuals.

These are children who are afraid
of the darkness
and the light
because their nightmares
don't only come at night.

K. Van Antwerp

Sunflower Seeds & Cigarettes

S he looked like a thirteen-year-old wearing too much make-up, not enough clothes, and no shoes. She smiled most of the time but when she spoke, it reminded me of the wind, quiet, hollow and chilling. Who was she, I wondered, with her too much make-up and not enough clothes. Why did she come to school with no shoes, and why, at the age of thirteen, did she not know how to read?

As the days passed, I began to see more and more of what this child was made of. Some things fascinated me and made me want to know more. Some things scared me and made me want to close my eyes. Scary movies make me want to close my eyes too. This, however, was not a movie, it was real. I began to understand why she was so thin. Sunflower seeds and cigarettes were all the nourishment she had. She shared her sunflower seeds, though, with everyone around her. She also shared her smile. One day she came into my office and shared her life. She had written it down actually, and had worked on writing it for many nights. Writing it wasn't enough, however, she wanted to tell me with her words. So I listened. It hurt. It actually hurt my ears. I could never tell the story as well as she wrote it.

"I was born in a hospital. I was 5 pounds 6 ounces. My mom loved me, but my dad I was not shure about. The monny my mom would made was

Reprinted from Reclaiming Children and Youth; Journal of Emotional and Behavioral Problems, published by PRO-ED, Austin, TX.

*wasted on pot and beer. When I came home from
the hospital there was no elextrisity or water. So
my mom brote me to Bunny's house and there she
took care of me. When I was three my parents got
a divorse. Me my mom and my brother was living
at Bunny's for one year. Then my mom meat a gye
named Sam. He was really nice at ferst. Then when
my mom married him he started hitting us and he
gave my brother black eyes. I ran away a lout that
is how I got into drugs and aclhas and cigerates.
I ran away down to North Hallewood I was prostituting. Me and Nancy meet a pimp and that is
how prostituting started. When we left the pimp
hit Nancy. Ever sence thaan I have never ran away.
Well my mom has Lisa devorses Sam we move and
now we are having a fun time."*

While she was talking I noticed the cigarette burns on her
arms and the strange scars on her legs. We talked about
the scars of her life's horrors on her body. She looked at
me with all the wisdom of a survivor of war and the smile
of a thirteen-year-old with too much make-up and not
enough clothes, and she said, "Oh yeah, that used to
happen to me a lot, but not now. I won't let it."

When I asked her why she told me this story, she simply
said, "You're the only one who's ever asked."

After that day I didn't need to ask why she wore too much
make-up and not enough clothes, or why she had no shoes.

I also didn't need to ask why she couldn't read. I knew all of these answers now. I didn't understand them, and I suppose I never really will. I did know just how important it was that this beautiful young girl learn how to read. I also knew how vital my role as a teacher was. To believe in her, to be patient with her, and most importantly, to accept her.

We worked together for almost a year. Then just as she had thanked me for asking before, she would thank me now for not asking–because she had to go. She had to leave again. Still with too much make-up, not enough clothes and no shoes. She did, however, know how to read a little bit better.

Annie left again to go back to the streets. It seemed she was gone almost over night. One year together had helped us both grow a lot. Annie learned 25 new basic sight words in reading and I learned, once again, the importance of knowing where a child spends the other eighteen hours of their day outside of school. This information gives invaluable insight into the short six hours they are in the classroom with us. The other eighteen hours in Annie's life were colorless, degrading and destructive. They did, however, help explain Annie's make-up, bare feet and cigarettes. Without this information, it would be extremely difficult to reach a child like Annie. I had two main objectives for working with Annie. The first was merely to gain an understanding and acceptance of this streetwise, school-phobic child. The second was academically based. I wanted to assess Annie's present level of academic performance and encourage her to further develop her skills. Most importantly, I wanted to focus on Annie's strengths, and use them to help me reach her. Although Annie's language arts skills were immature, she had developed a love for this subject. The interesting thing about getting students excited about writing is that it arouses their curiosity about interrelated subjects such as reading and spelling.

Annie became very focused, she wanted to write. She wanted to be able to express herself and get all her bottled up feelings out onto paper. Allowing Annie to write about her life on the streets of North Hollywood was exactly what she needed.

I wasn't able to change Annie's life during our time together. I wasn't able to take away her scars or burns, and I certainly wasn't able to prevent her from leaving again.

I was, however, able to listen, to help her feel accepted and to teach her more than she ever knew about writing. Or at least that's what she told me the last time we worked together.

Scars

Carlos is big and quiet like a statue. He never smiles but he silently protects students smaller than he. Carlos remembers his life by the scars he wears on his skin. Big scars. Two on his face, one on his arm, and another across his chest. Carlos is only fifteen, with so many scars.

By fourteen years old he had already begun to take the pain from these scars and use it to hurt other children. Carlos was scary. Other students feared Carlos and his quietness. Teachers also feared Carlos.

Carlos was quiet, but his scars told a story, a story that Carlos wanted to write. It explained Carlos, his scars and his silence.

"I was Bron on 1-18-79 And I was the Frist Kid I lived in California all my life when I was three. I got hit by A toaster on the head And I 5 we went to Mexico to my Anuts house, And one week befor we left I got Pushed into A Rosebush And When I was 8 my mom had my bother And four of my unlcs got busted they did 3 year in pision And that night I seen the most monye in my life they had Five paper bag And they had the most guns I ever seen to After All that happened the next day my dad And my unlcs wet to take monye to my unlcs And when I truned 11 two of y unlcs came out And I

truned 12 my ohter two unlce came out And when I truned 13 the day of my birthday I got two cuts on my face. When I truned 14 1 week After my brithday I stabed some guy in the back. And After that I started going to this school."

Carlos was a challenge. It is difficult trying to teach a child who is inside the body of a man full of scars. After Carlos wrote his story I understood his scars. Each one of them represented some important incident in Carlos's life. As a teacher, I wasn't exactly sure how to help Carlos open up, but I knew it was important.

One day, Carlos missed the bus and had to stay after class waiting for a ride. I asked Carlos if he would help me paint a picture. Carlos agreed. As we began to paint, Carlos began to talk. He drew a picture of a little boy floating on a sailboat in the middle of a beautiful blue ocean. His sky had marshmallow clouds, a bright yellow sun, and birds flying peacefully by. Carlos talked about his life and his scars. He also spoke of the dreams he just drew.

Although it was almost the end of the school year, I was able to spend a few more afternoons painting and conversing with Carlos. I'm not sure if either one of us knew exactly what was happening while we were painting, but it seemed to be a very comfortable form of communication.

The pictures Carlos continued to draw were similar to the first: colorful, playful and innocent. These pictures were quite a contrast to his life and the stories he told as he drew them. I listened to his stories and I commented on his artwork. The only connection I made between the two was his strong need for expression.

He had dreams, he had goals, and he had a lot of scars. It was difficult to tell whether the dreams or the scars would guide his future. Art therapy, I discovered, was the key that would help Carlos unlock his silence.

Once we began to unlock Carlos's world of dreams through art, we began, slowly, to write these ideas onto paper. We began to create "A Book of Dreams." Each dream was connected to a picture and each picture was connected to a feeling. This book personalized both writing and art for Carlos. It became something tangible. Something Carlos could hold onto and look at, but most importantly it became something Carlos could share.

Carlos was creative, and his ability to compose words and pictures inspired me. It inspired me to grasp onto this talent and use it to help this young man reach out to the world around him.

When Carlos went to high school, I collected his portfolio of pictures and gave this invaluable key to his next teacher.

Motel Eleven

Jessica's eyelashes stood out like a model's on the page of a magazine. Her eyeliner was black and drew dramatic lines around her eyes. Mysterious eyes. Dramatic eyes. Beautiful Cleopatra eyes. Jessica, an eleven-year-old with eyes beyond her years.

She loved school, it made her laugh and it allowed her to be eleven years old. She came to school almost everyday, walking through the streets of her neighborhood, which were rough and crowded. Some days Jessica got swallowed up by those rough streets and rough crowds. It was on those days that our classroom felt a little empty. In school Jessica sat at a table with four other students. She was the youngest one at the table, but her stories and her eyes kept everyone's attention.

Writing was Jessica's favorite subject. She wanted to put her words onto paper. Writing stories made her Cleopatra eyes light up. The other students in class enjoyed her stories too. Jessica's stories were like a radio show, people gathered around to listen. One day Jessica was gone. It was as if someone had moved the dial and we could no longer find the station. After a few days I began calling Jessica's house. No one seemed to know where she was. Eleven years old, and no one knew? It was as if no one really cared.

I cared, and I tried to find Jessica and her dancing eyes. Then one day she called on the phone. She wanted to come back, sit at the round table and tell stories. So she did. Her eyes looked different. Her make-up was gone and silence was all that could be heard. She wrote a few stories, she shared none.

Finally, one day she left this story on her desk after school.

When she was eleven years old she started hanging around with the wrong crowd. One day she went to a party with her friends. And her so called friends left her at the hotel room by herself. They thought she would be safe there alone. When they went back for her they were too late. She had been raped already. ·

And now she lives with the shame of her past. After that happened she stopped hanging around with cholas and cholos. She changed her lifestyle and now she regrets ever going to that party. So she now lives with the shame of her miserable life.

She tries to act like nothing ever happened. But deep down inside is where she hurts.

After she left that story, Jessica didn't return to school for a few days. I called her everyday and talked about the story. It took almost two weeks to hear her voice again.

She was eleven years old, raped by four men and left in a

motel room. She felt ashamed, so she quit coming to school, quit telling stories and quit wearing make-up on her eyes. The story she left on her desk, was written in third person. She was an eleven-year-old who would never again see through the same eyes. And we would never again see the beauty that once danced in those eyes.

I got Jessica to return to school eventually, and we began a slow process of finding her. This process began with daily visits to the school counselor. We arranged about 15 minutes a day, to begin when Jessica arrived on campus, to help her find her confidence. When she came into the classroom, Jessica was given time to write in a personal journal for at least 10 minutes. This writing was only being used as a quiet form of expression. These were not stories or words Jessica needed to share. She knew I would only read them if asked. Most days she asked–which was an important form of communication for her.

Rape counseling was the next step Jessica needed to take. Her story format, which used the third person, and her attempts to put the past behind her concerned me. We contacted a local Rape Crisis Center for adolescents and arranged some meetings. The counselor came to school to meet with Jessica, where she felt safe.

Following through with the police report and deciding to press charges was the most difficult process for this eleven-year-old. We worked very closely with a team of professionals and her family to complete this step.

We worked together–counselor, teacher and child, side by side, for the next eight months. When summer came, Jessica (or Cleopatra as I will always remember her) moved to another state. I hope she will continue to find power in writing and I hope her eyes will, some day, dance again.

Expelled

Fifteen years old with seven weapons, a lot of pain and a large black jacket. His life was not worth living, so he hid under his jacket. He was in class everyday, but we never saw his face. We only saw his jacket. It was dark, big and safe underneath Marcos's jacket. This was not only where Marcos hid, but where he thought about his life.

The Story of My Life

"It started when I was Boren. I was a little Bady and I was small my mom and Dad took care of me. But mostly my mom Because my Dad was working All Day and all night. When I terned The Age 2 I started walking very well Then when I terned The Age 10 my mom started geting mean She was in so much stress with the Bills and her life that she Abused me a little and took every thing out on me. She All so Did to my sister to. Then one Day my Dad came early from work and ssaw that she was hiting me with A metel part of the Belt And scared me. My Dad Quckly Pushed my mom away from me and told me to go To the shower. When I was standing in The Bathroom my Brother was Telling me what happed. Then my Dad told me to go in The shower and he will talk to my mom. After I came out of the shower I saw

that my mom was leaving I said Dont leave will talk about it Then we Did And she and me agreed in not hiting me when she mad. Then when my mom hit my sister and she was crying I told my Dad and my Dad got mad at my mom. Then she got mad and put me in a cold Bathtube And hit me with a bar of Sope. And I Didn't Tell anybody thill I was 12 years old. And it was to late couse my Dad and mom Duvoresed. And now I fell like I Don't have a famly couse my Dad is Allways work and my mom is living in L.A. And now I got A girlfreand and I going To school new clows I feel good And that is the sory of my life."

Marcos was expelled from school for hitting another student over the head with a crowbar and carrying seven weapons onto campus: two knives, one crowbar, one screwdriver, one knuckle ring, one rock, one black jacket, and one child with a hole in his heart. The story of his life helped me understand the motivation for his weapons.

Marcos was one of those children who was silent–with so much to say. I saw the words in Marcos's eyes when he took his jacket off one day. He was fourteen and near the end of his life. He sniffed glue, locked himself in closets and tried to kill himself three times.

I knew Marcos wanted to tell his story, not take his life. I also knew he told stories best when he drew pictures. The day Marcos left for the hospital, I made sure he had a pad of paper and a new box of crayons.

At the very young age of fifteen, Marcos was placed in a psychiatric hospital, diagnosed with manic depression. His ninth grade teacher came to see me with a letter and a questionnaire sent by his doctor. She sat down, with near tears in her eyes, and asked me if I ever felt that I knew Marcos. I shared with her the stories Marcos had written and the art work he had done. I told her what his eyes had looked like the day he took off his jacket, and I told her about the day his father came to school. He came to school with Marcos by his side to explain to me that he had to put Marcos into a hospital.

As a teacher, I knew that exact moment was the time to make Marcos feel something good inside. With Marcos's permission I shared his art work and some of his writing with his father. His father had never been to school before, he'd never heard anything positive about his son. He began to cry and hug Marcos. Marcos just stared at me.

Although I'm not a therapist, I certainly knew that one way to reach Marcos was through writing. I shared this with his new teacher, who would be working with Marcos in the hospital. I also explained the importance of accepting Marcos and looking at his silence as a form of communication. If given the opportunity to draw and write to express his feelings, one day Marcos would emerge from under his jacket.

In our classroom I had used Marcos's work as his voice. I displayed it on the walls and shared it with others. In doing this, I discovered a way to help Marcos lift his eyes, lift his head, and show interest in the world around him.

I felt good about the time Marcos and I shared together. I felt a connection. By using the information obtained through Marcos' writing, I was able to help others understand this silent child.

The Girl Who Could Smile But Did Not

She was thirteen years old, pregnant and black. She had rows of beautiful braids in her hair and a delicate face that never had the chance to smile. I wondered what had made her lose her smile and if she would ever find it again. Like finding a lost puppy, the loss is overwhelming but when it is found, your heart can't stop beating. I wanted her heart to beat. I wanted her to smile. We worked together. We talked. We read. We figured out all the problems in history, but we never smiled together. Time drew nearer for her to have her baby. For the first time all year, I saw her expression change. Her eyes turned to gray. Not smoke gray or blue gray. An ugly gray. Her thoughts and ideas began to shift, and her disposition defined sadness. She was having a baby. I guess this idea made her begin to think of her childhood. One day she sat down and wrote about her childhood. These were a few of her memories.

"When I was growing up as a child I did not have a very good childhood. So many horrible things happened to my mom, my brother and I. My father was not the type of man that somebody would want to be married to. He took medicine for epileptic seizures, he drank alcohol and used drugs and on tops of that he picked up other women and was very violent.

As a child I was beat, and my mom went through

physical and mental abuse. My brother and I got whoopings for nothing. If my mom tried to step in she would get hit to. He spoiled me and I got away with just about everything, but that still did not matter. My mom did not know about the abuse and molestation because it took place while she was at work. My brother and I were told not to say anything about it or else we would get it. So the abuse went on.

My brother had these two friends next door. My brother an I used to go swimming with them. When we would get out of the pool we would go back to my house to dry off in my room. So one day my dad came in their and made my brother and I leave the room. When we walked out he closed the door behind us. He was in there for a while with my two friends.

When I was four years old my cousin came over in the morning so that she could get a ride to school. I was in the bathroom washing off and I called her into the bathroom and I started telling her everything that my dad was doing to me. I guess he was standing by the door listening because when I got ready to walk out of the bath- room and go into my room to put my clothes on, he called me into the room. He told me to take my gown off and he started whooping me with a belt.

It was hurting so bad I turt my face up towards him so he would stop. He told me to turn my face back or he was going to hit me again. I didn't turn my face because I wanted him to stop, but instead of stopping he hit me in my face with the belt.

After he was done whooping me he tried to put alcohol on my face so the swelling would go down but it didn't one side of my face was swollen bad. When my brother, my cousin, my mom and I were in the living room getting ready to leave, I showed my mom what my dad did to me and from that day forward we never went back to our house."

When she finished talking I knew the definition of her childhood: the past 12 years of life that had taken her smile.

A year after we met, the man who had taken her smile with a belt was killed in a prison. It was then that I think I saw her smile. If only for just one second.

Although her life was full of abuse, molestation and scars, pregnancy was the only thing that caused teachers and counselors to stand up and notice this bright thirteen-year-old child. Her story is a perfect example of children who quietly display, but deeply suffer from, factors that place them at-risk. Straight A's and a beautiful face allowed this child to go unnoticed by individuals trained to work with children. Not until she became pregnant and was placed into a program for at-risk youth, did this child ever have a voice. Writing gave her a voice. She felt free andconfident with a pen in her hand.

After she wrote her childhood memories, she turned to me and said, *"I want to write more, I want to write to magazines and have these stories published. If other kids read my story they may find the courage to write their own, or at least feel like they're not alone."*

So we began to stay after school, write on the computer, compile stories and write to magazine editors. These stories covered subjects from abuse and molestation to teenage pregnancy and motherhood. We read a variety of books on these subjects together and we worked closely with counselors. The most important thing we did, however, was write.

Before summer ended, I sat down with her next teacher. We discussed the experiences and growth which had occurred through the writing process. She agreed to continue to encourage this form of communication because even though this child did not appear to be at-risk, her childhood memories told a different story.

Kam

S he had sunflowers on her dress, and when she twirled in circles those sunflowers seemed to dance. She was six years old and didn't like to wear shoes. One day she was left standing beside her sister on the roadside. Just like two ice cream cones melting in the sun. Alone. No one ever came back to pick her up. So she came to school with sunflowers on her dress and started to sing.

We sang together all day long. It was nice, our music–it was free. I could tell she felt the freedom down to her toes. That was probably the reason she never wore her shoes. Then slowly the music began to get interrupted. They would quietly come and take her hand and walk her out of the classroom to go on a visit.

I wasn't sure who she was visiting, all I knew was each time the music was interrupted, we lost a little piece of the feeling. The freedom slipped away. When she came back to class her sunflowers no longer danced. I could no longer see her smile–only a pair of shoes in the middle of the floor with no one inside them. It was then, after the visits, that she would hide. I would see her curled up under a table or stuffed into a bookcase like a book that is too big for the bookshelf.

Each time she'd hide I'd quietly go to her side and tell her to use her words just like our music, to express herself. Feel free, let your words be like the sunflowers twirling on your dress.

She only cried and listened and sat very still. One day they came to get her for a visit. This time she put on her shoes, walked to the door and said: *"You don't under-stand—I don't like my daddy. He whoops me, he locks me in closets and he hurts me. I don't want to visit him. You visit him if you want to. I hate him and I won't visit him."*

Then she took off her shoes and began to dance.

Kam was only in my classroom for six months. Time lines make work more focused and motivating. I was motivated to reach Kam. I wanted to hold on to the small piece of happiness I saw in her dancing. To reach Kam in her world of fears, I started each and every morning with music. I allowed Kam to kick off her shoes and dance. When she wanted to sing, we sang nice and loud. Music was a comfort for Kam, a way to feel good inside.

Kam was a unique child with very individual needs. To teach Kam, I needed to reach her through music and dancing. So our classroom curriculum included music. We used music in a variety of ways. We incorporated it into language arts, science, math and health. We even listened to music during lunch and P.E. Music also became a way for Kam to communicate her thoughts and feelings. As we listened to the words and songs written by others, Kam wanted to write a song of her own. So one day she drew a picture and wrote these words:

Wen I dans and I sing I feel beautifl insid it takes
away my tears
nothing can mak me cri.
Kam

The words to this song explained why the sunflowers twirled on Kam's dress every time she heard music. It explained how singing put sunshine into her life, and how music must be a part of her life, and curriculum everyday.

Incorporating children's music into the classroom curriculum is a fabulous way to reach many different students. Music can have lyrics which teach academics, cross cultural borders and empower children to communicate.

This communication can occur through oral language, artistic drawings or personal writing. Writing a song gave this six-year-old the opportunity to "feel beautiful inside".

Snickers

Snickers–a little nutty–that's what they said he was. He was eight years old, had riveting brown eyes and was a little bit nutty. I didn't believe them, I didn't believe he was nutty. He had eight years of life, none of which had been worth living. He had a very creative mind, a body that would not sit still and a very loud voice. I liked him. I liked him the first day I met him. He was easy to like, but difficult to understand.

When they walked him to my classroom they pushed him through the doorway, rolled their eyes and whispered, "SED." SED; the most widely misused acronym in the field of education. SED, I was taught, meant "seriously emotionally disturbed." After years in the field of special education I personally changed the meaning of those horrid letters. SED to me means "seriously emotionally damaged."

Snickers was not disturbed, he was damaged. When people look at an individual as disturbed, that individual becomes the problem. Snickers was not the problem, the people who sexually abused him, burned him with cigarettes and beat him daily were emotionally disturbed.

Snickers was a beautiful eight year old child who had been damaged. It is important to see this difference, because then educators have a much clearer path to reaching a child like Snickers.

I call him Snickers because of his laugh: wild, carefree, continuous and loud. How did this child ever learn to laugh? That's what fascinated me about Snickers, he had an interesting love of life. You could see this love, along with every other emotion through his solid brown eyes. Those eyes, which appeared to cover half his face, made me curious.

His academic history and school performance did not reflect a very positive picture. Snickers was a classic reject. Rejected from program after program and moved from foster home to foster home. I stopped counting the number of locations after eight. One for each year of his life was enough to make me shudder.

The referral to our program simply stated, "disrupted placement." I knew my time with Snickers was limited because this was, after all, an emergency shelter care program. Students were enrolled from two days to two weeks or at the outer-most limits, a few months. Working within this time frame, I knew I would not change the world for Snickers, but I did believe I could at least meet him somewhere between his world and mine, and hold his hand.

Reaching Snickers was hard work. I don't think I did reach him completely the first time he went through our program. However, after another "disrupted placement," he came back a second time. This time he stayed a lot longer and I did find a way to hold his hand.

We developed a late start program for Snickers. He liked

to sleep in a little bit in the morning and he liked to eat breakfast alone. Snickers was not a morning person. This personality trait is common to many people. Because he was a child, however, no one would accept it. He would be forced to wake up, participate and behave. I truly believe that was part of Snickers' history of early morning problems in school. With a late start, approximately 20 to 30 minutes extra time to "get it together" in the morning, Snickers did remarkably better in school.

When Snickers arrived, the classroom activities were already underway. This gave him the opportunity to jump right in. Some people describe his "jumping-in" as an attention disorder. I saw it as a love of learning and a curiosity to see what was next.

Snickers appeared to enjoy music tremendously while he worked. I think it gave him the opportunity to use his voice without being told to be quiet. We listened to a lot of music and sang together out loud.

Dinosaurs and science fiction figures fascinated Snickers. He would read, write, draw and describe these amazing creatures by the hour. Mathematics was another subject that held his interest. He loved to be challenged to use his brain.

His brain. How did it work exactly? This was a question which intrigued me daily. It seemed to move so rapidly and so productively in its own way. Two things I did learn about this beautiful child while we were together, were his hunger for the human touch and his need to be understood.

I patted him on the back or shoulder, physically sat by his side and often gave him a hug to let him know he was not alone. I also gave him the opportunity to write. He used this opportunity, and his words were honest and sad.

"My mom used drugs wen I was a bady. In her stomch. I was born addicted to drugs. My mom had a rougf funnie voice from taking her drugs. My dad scares me. Did you kno he puts cigeretts on my body all the time. He is scary like the mean drunk mans. It is bad to do drugs they will hurt your bady. My foster mom broke my brain by smashing my head and pinching my nek. I must be a bad bady because my mom didnt wnt to keep me she only wanted to drink and smoke. When your mom does drugs you have to go to a new hose and try a new famly who will not hurt you. I didntt find them yet. Maybe my mom is better now and wants me home. But not my dad he is scarey. I miss my famly."

Snickers and I read this story together out loud. We talked about drugs, alcohol, cigarettes and foster families. We talked about these subjects everyday. We tried to understand why he didn't have a family and we tried, together, to make our time at school as warm as a fresh loaf of bread, baked at home with a family.

The Dog He Left Behind

He walked to class with his pants too big, his shoes untied and his hair sticking up as if it had been sucked through a vacuum. He was seven years old and didn't show his smile. His sister was five. His brother was ten. They didn't show their smiles either. Anger, rage and hurt was all they could show the first few days we met. He sat with his five year old sister at a big yellow table, while his ten year old brother sat at a blue one. I wonder if Jake picked the yellow table so he could have a little sunshine in his life. Their mom and dad had both overdosed on heroin the night before they came into our classroom. Lou was ten and he knew his parents did drugs. Shannon was five and all she knew was that mommy was not with her today. Jake was seven and very confused.

Jake, Shannon and Lou were alone, but at least they had each other. They had each other to help understand the violence and anger they felt inside. They didn't communicate with words, they communicated by kicking, punching and biting. In less than one day our classroom had become quite a battle ground. Shannon, five years old and tiny, was the loudest in her war cries. Lou was quiet and very subtle in his ways, and Jake drew pictures of blood and death each and every day.

When Jake brought me his first picture I almost had to

close my eyes. His picture had eight people, three on the ground, four with guns and one who towered above them all with guns, knives and fire coming out of his head. Everyone in the picture was killing or being killed. When I asked Jake what this picture was, he just rolled his eyes and said, "It's my family." Jake didn't do any more with that picture, he just asked me to keep it. The next day Jake drew a picture of three boys playing outside. One boy had a gun and the other two were running. Jake said, *"This is a picture of me killing my friends, their names are Michael and Chase and I'm killing them because they make fun of me and they deserve it. They're dead now, so bye."*

Jake wanted this picture to hang on the wall. So it did.

Three days after we met, I walked into the gymnasium to see Jake sitting in the corner crying. When I sat down beside him I asked him why he was sad. He didn't answer, he only cried harder. I asked him if I could help him, if something had happened at school. He only cried. I asked him if he was hurt on the outside, or maybe the inside. It was then that he lifted his eyes and looked at me. I reached out to hold his hand and I asked him if he missed his mom. He wiped his tears on his sleeve and said, "I miss my mom, I miss my dad and I miss my dog Brownie. I wonder if Brownie's dead."

Since my class was in P.E. and it was my lunch time, I knew Jake and I could have some quiet time alone. So I said, "Let's go back to class and make a card for every one you miss." "Even Brownie?" he asked. "Especially Brownie." I said. When we got to class Jake picked out three pieces of colored paper. He asked me to write some words on the board, "Mom", "Dad", "Brownie" and "I miss you." I turned some music on, pulled up a chair and quietly ate my yogurt while Jake sat beside the window at the big yellow table making cards for people he missed. Jake began to talk while he made his cards. His words were the key to his fears. He said, *"Me and Shannon and Lou were sleeping when the policeman came into our house and woke us up. When we were walking out of our room I saw my mommy and daddy sleeping too, on the floor. My uncle Rockie was there yelling at the policeman. My uncle Rockie always makes everyone's nose bleed. He punches em' really hard and their noses bleed. He punches my aunt Ruthie's nose a lot. She's always crying with my mom. I don't know why I'm here or really where I am. I don't know where my mom and dad are either. I wonder if my uncle Rockie will feed my dog Brownie, I hope my mom or dad calls soon.*

"When Jake finished his cards he stopped talking. "There," he said "What do these cards say?" They all said, "I miss you Brownie."

Just then the rest of the class came back, and the boy with his hair sticking up and I hung his three cards to Brownie on the classroom wall.

Three months after we met, Jake, Lou and Shannon were

leaving. They were going to a foster home. Jake was scared, yet the last three pictures he drew had a flower, a sun and a school.

There were no people in these pictures and there was no killing.

No One Ever Notices His Shoes

They're too big, they're untied, and the soles are worn out, but no one ever notices his shoes. I never thought it was that simple to make someone smile, but when I noticed his shoes, he did.

I started to tie them, because that's what you do when a child's shoes are untied. He stopped reading and slowly lifted his eyes from the book. He said, *"My mom never tied my shoes. She was always drunk. I don't even think she could if she tried. My dad probably would of tied my shoes but he's in jail. My dad loves to watch football, he would never miss a football game but now he misses lots of games because he's in jail."*

"I was living with my mom but she never tied my shoes, she only hit me when my shoes were untied."

"Oh well, someday I know my dad will probably tie my shoes when he gets out of jail."

He turned his eyes back to his story. I continued to tie his shoes. I wanted them to fit, I wanted them to be tied and I wanted the soles to be brand new.

As I quietly stood up to walk away he raised his eyes again, *"Thank you."* he said, *"For noticing my shoes."*

"You're welcome."

Not only did Taylor's shoes go unnoticed, he went unnoticed. Taylor's mother was like an ice cube, floating around, soaking up alcohol. Taylor's dad sometimes called from jail.

They don't know that Taylor is ten years old and doesn't know how to add. He knows the alphabet but doesn't know how to write words. He loves stories but can't read them, and his shoes are untied, but he can't tie them.

Because of all this frustration, Taylor is scared, angry and hurt. He acts out in class by yelling, tearing up his work, and assaulting his teachers and classmates. Taylor has been labeled Seriously Emotionally Disturbed (SED). His school records indicate that Taylor has severe learning disabilities and a history of violence. He has lived in a variety of residential treatment programs and foster homes. Taylor does not have a home. He has anger and untied shoes. His life is a number of uncertainties, and he has no skills to communicate his fears.

Taylor's psychological evaluation discusses the fact that Taylor "will not make eye contact with anyone". I wonder if they ever noticed Taylors' shoes–his eyes never left mine when I stopped to tie them.

As Taylor's teacher, it was my responsibility to discover why Taylor was using violence to communicate, and to help him find an alternative functionally-equivalent behavior. Tying Taylor's shoes was the first step in reaching him. I <u>noticed</u> <u>him</u>. I took the time to care about his well being and his shoelaces.

From that day forward Taylor and I had a different relationship. We had connected on some level. Now that I had Taylor's trust and eye contact, I used it to reach him academically and socially. Our lessons were a form of personal interaction between myself, Taylor, and other students. We gave Taylor a "buddy" to help him with academics and we found alternative ways to express frustration–through words.

Taylor was only in our program a short period of time. He never hit another person, he did make eye contact, and his shoes were always tied.

Taylor did not go unnoticed.

The Window

4:30 arrives and she waits by the elevator, looking out the window into the parking lot. She spends her days now looking through windows. Waiting. Her baby weighs two pounds and lives behind the glass inside an incubator. Waiting. Waiting to be held, waiting to go home. Waiting to have a mother.

A mother–what is a mother? Well, she's a mother now. An 18-year-old single mother. What does that mean? Using heroin? Abandoning children to survive under a bridge? Spending time in jail? Allowing your children to be molested? That's the only example of motherhood she ever knew. Now her baby weighs two pounds and she has to be a mother. So she waits beside the elevator looking out the window for me. I was coming to see the baby. I was coming to look through the window with her and talk about being a mother.

I've never been a mother but I had a different definition of motherhood to share with her. We looked through the window for what seemed like hours. We weren't seeing the baby. We were seeing her life. It felt like a winter night before a storm, when you hurry to shut the window. It was cold, empty and dark, the window to her soul. But we had to leave the window open and look through it.

She remembered being seven years old and living under

a bridge with her older brother Freddy. Freddy was eight, one year older than she. When they found her and her brother, she did not talk. Freddy did all the talking. She was taken from under the bridge and placed in her grandparents' home. When she was 13, "they" had to come back and take her away again. She was being molested. This time when they found her, she needed to talk for herself and take care of herself. There was no big brother to take care of her.

Then, at age 13 she faced the world. Alone. Shelter care, group homes and foster homes. Homes. Ironic choice of a word–none of them were ever home to her. It actually felt safer under the bridge with her big brother by her side. Now he's gone too.

Now there's only me and a few other strangers to help her understand. Understand that "they" were actually trying to help her. She shared her feelings about her situation with me. *"I wish I never told. I wish I'd kept my mouth shut. Because then maybe, just maybe, I'd still have a family. He still has a family you know, my Grandfather. I was told I'd be protected if I told. I was told I would be safe and he could no longer climb through my bedroom window at night. But you know what? He's actually the one who's protected. He's surrounded by family and friends. And me, well I'm alone, surrounded by strangers...funny, I don't even have my own bedroom window anymore."*

We left our spot by the window. She was tired now. Tired of looking through windows. We went to dinner together. She didn't eat her meal. She still had the habit of saving it for her brother in case he was hungry. We drove home in silence. She had a very long day ahead of her tomorrow, looking through windows at her baby. She never finished high school. She doesn't have a job and she wishes she didn't have a two pound baby.

PART TWO

At-Risk Children

Statistics show that the number of children entering our public school system today who are homeless, hungry, abused, neglected, pregnant, illiterate, and suicidal is growing rapidly. Being able to identify these children and understand the factors involved in their lives that place them at-risk will help both students and educators deal more effectively with these challenges. The most natural place for these children to be cared for is by their families; however, many of these families are dysfunctional and fragmented. These children are alone and scared, and have little support. Although the scope of this problem is too broad for the educational system to handle alone, school programs provide an appropriate place to start. Schools in many ways have become the care takers of these children, yet in order to do so effectively, educators need to learn who at-risk children are and how to better understand them.

Some of the most common factors associated with students considered educationally at-risk are:

- ▲ poverty
- ▲ low grades/low achievement
- ▲ absenteeism
- ▲ behavior problems
- ▲ retention
- ▲ suspensions
- ▲ language barriers

According to research, these factors can reliably predict, as early as third grade, which students will drop out of school and which students will stay. Because of the problems at-risk students confront on a daily basis, both at home and in school, they seem to be caught in a cycle which denies them success in school. At-risk children often enter school with skills that are behind those of other children academically, and they continue to fall farther and farther behind. Teachers are in a position to have significant impact on the cognitive and emotional development of these children.

Research has shown that at-risk children bring a variety of assets to the classroom. By using the strategies at-risk children bring into the classroom, teachers can help support and accelerate the learning process. These include interest and curiosity in oral and artistic expression; as well as a previously undiscovered ability to learn through manipulation of appropriate learning materials and through interesting applications. At-risk children often also have the capability to delve eagerly into intrinsically interesting tasks, and a capacity for learning to write prior to mastering reading skills.

The strategies that schools can use to ameliorate the conditions of at-risk students must include collaboration with families and communities. It is difficult for schools to be effective when they work in isolation from the familial, cultural, and community context of the children they serve. Good pedagogy begins with the strengths and experiences of its students. Based upon this precept, I incorporated a writing curriculum into the classroom which allowed students to choose writing topics that were meaningful and authentic to them as learners. The outcome of this writing curriculum is the collection of stories included in this book. These stories were written or orally communicated by children who are considered at-risk in today's society. It is their "voice", their crying out of how they perceive life to be.

Writing Curriculum Guide

Language arts, which includes both the written and verbal forms of language, can be used as a tool for communication as well, as these stories demonstrate, as a source of empowerment for at-risk students. As children come into the classroom they bring with them stories, songs, language and other cultural activities that help them construct their social lives. Unfortunately, schools often fail to connect this outside culture to the culture of school. Research studies have shown that bridging the gap between the outside culture and the school is one of the most important strategies necessary to reach at-risk students. By accepting a child's way of speaking or writing about the events in his personal life, teachers help bridge the gap between the most prominent cultures in a child's world.

The collection of stories included in this book were written by children in today's society who are at-risk for failure, not only in school but in life as well. These stories came into being through instructional strategies implemented on a daily basis in a curricular activity entitled "Writing Workshop". Traditionally, these stories would have been returned to the students rife with red ink corrections, highlighting spelling, punctuation, capitalization and grammar errors. Possibly deemed unacceptable due to content. Probably exhibiting an unfavorable grade. This overwhelmingly discouraging process will result in a students refusal to participate in writing assignments. These children, intimidated and afraid of feeling failure are likely to display disruptive behavior. The foremost objective of the educator in this situation is to encourage the student to engage in writing activities. Then, and only then, is it possible to begin developing their language arts skills.

Writing Workshop is a twenty to thirty minute academic activity based on the sociocognitive and personal formats of teaching writing. The sociocognitive and personal formats of teaching writing provide methods to reach students who are so discouraged with writing they have put down the pen. Both of these methods encourage students to draw upon their memories, dreams, observations, life experience and expectations to make the writing experience meaningful and authentic. Sociocognitive and personal writing allows students to use their own voice to communicate with the world around them. It allows them to be creative, fresh and genuine.

The teacher's role in this process is to guide, prompt, encourage and care for the students. The basic principles or guidelines for sociocognitive and personal writing instruction are as follows:

▲ *Allow writing topics to be socially based* so children learn to develop literacy in ways which represent the environments they come from. This can be incorporated into the curriculum on a daily basis in the form of personal journals or writing portfolios.

▲ *Allow writing to connect to the students background knowledge* by incorporating personal topics into lessons such as autobiographies, family events and life experiences. This technique will increase a child's fluency and competence in writing.

▲ *Allow students to interact during the writing process.* This will increase their involvement and learning. This interaction can include both peers and teachers.

▲ *Help students to learn component skills within the context of the writing text.* This becomes a three-phase writing task which includes a rough draft, a second draft and a final draft. The rough draft enables students to discover and disclose their thoughts without fear of criticism. The second and final drafts give students time to proofread and learn about editing.

▲ *Allow students to approach writing as a problem-solving process.* This will enable them to develop competence in writing while addressing their individual personal difficulties. Writing about personal life events is a way for at-risk students to express themselves and help solve problems in their lives.

▲ *Allow students to use personal writing topics as a voice to connect with the world around them.*

▲ *Allow students opportunities to write extended text.* Extended text such as poetry, journal entries, letters, reports, and stories are instructional formats which help children develop competence.

There are fundamental beliefs about both writing and learning that go beyond exposure to the principles and techniques of the sociocognitive and personal writing formats. Educators schooled in skill-based perspective need to discover these beliefs to successfully implement this writing curriculum. Although the number of at-risk students in today's public schools is growing rapidly, it is unjust to write off children who are homeless, abused and who suffer from the other at-risk conditions as unteachable. Strategies such as the sociocognitive and personal formats of writing exist to lessen the effects of the at-risk child's conditions. Writing is their voice–please listen.

Afterword

Children who are abused, neglected, homeless, drug addicted, suicidal, pregnant and uneducated are defined as at-risk children. This burgeoning population of children is entereing our school systems at an alarming rate.

Understanding the term "at-risk" and how it defines the lives of so many young children, is the first step to reaching them. An educator's responsibility is no longer limited to academic instruction but also encompasses a childs' social and emotional development. Schools must provide consistency, stability and role models for these children.

The sociocognitive and personal formats of writing instruction outlined in this book present teachers with curricular/instructional methods which will help them better understand at-risk children. These methods, if incorporated on a daily basis, empower students both as learners and individuals.

The stories collected in this book were written by at-risk children and provide valuable insight into their lives and their need for communication. The student/teacher interactions described in each story outline instructional methods and strategies which can be incorporated into the classroom.

Teachers who have incorporated these writing practices

into their curriculum have reported an increase in both student interest and academic output. Children who were reluctant to write began writing when the topic emphasized their experiences and gave value to their lives. Moreover, this instruction helps build understanding, respect and trust between teachers and their students.

Teachers have concerns regarding issues disclosed by children when writing about their personal lives. Educators are concerned that if they incorporate this writing process without the support of administrators and counselors, they may be confronted with difficult issues they may not feel competent to handle, such as abuse, molestation, neglect, depression and violence.

These questions and concerns are legitimate. They speak to the need for more training in the area of at-risk children and in the area of child abuse detection and prevention. If teachers have support and resources to help deal with the difficult issues these children present, they will feel more comfortable and confident when dealing with them in the classroom.

To work successfully with at-risk students, teachers need to understand both the term "at-risk" and the characteristics commonly associated with these students. School districts need to provide in-services and training that outline various teaching methods that have been successful with at-risk children.

Children with difficult life situations need to have a place to go where they can feel safe and trusting of the adults around them. Once these children make this connection through writing they will begin to grow and develop in a wide range of academic areas. Their minds will be able to focus on other aspects of the world around them.

At-risk children are good people in bad lives. They have been hurt and need to be heard. Schools are a wonderful place to begin reaching out to these children and offering them a place to be heard. Writing addresses this need and provides opportunities for communication. If teachers in the public school system could be trained in the sociocognitive and personal formats of writing, they could use these methods on a daily basis. If this occurred, educators would better understand the children in their classrooms, and more children in the public schools would succeed. At-risk children, when given a tool for communication and people who listen, become children with hope.

A word of encouragement to those who are embarking on a career with children. You have before you a challenge and a unique opportunity to make our classrooms a place where children are not only seen, but heard; not only heard but understood and accepted. May you have the courage to help each child who suffers, and draw strength from each triumph, large and small.

About the Author

Kathleen Van Antwerp grew up in the San Fernando Valley in Southern California. She began working with children after graduating from high school and continued to do so while attending California State University, Northridge. She received a bachelor's degree in Child Development as a Child Mental Health Specialist and a Master's degree in Special Education. Kathleen has taught severely emotionally disturbed children, high-risk junior high school students in a California community school, and abused, neglected and abandoned children, grades K-6 in an emergency shelter. Working as a Behavioral Specialist, Kathleen has assisted developmentally disabled and emotionally damaged children who have been placed in foster care.

It was in these settings that the lives of these children so moved the author that she dedicated this book to their words; seldom spoken, rarely heard, remarkably poignant. She recognized that these children frequently were unable to read, unable to write, and likely unable to raise their voices above the din of their lives.

Kathleen continues to be involved with helping children on many levels–a rare combination of compassion, knowledge and skill. She remains committed to working with the children who have so enriched her life.

Watch for Kathleen Van Antwerp's upcoming book:

HIDDEN UPSTAIRS
Stories of Emotional Damage

Comments?

We at Quiet Thunder Publishing are committed to providing you with the highest quality, most informative publications available.

If you have any comments, suggestions or questions of any kind regarding this book, or a related issue, we would like to hear from you.

Director of Publications
Quiet Thunder Publishing
P.O. Box 2097
Ventura, CA 93002

"I Can't Come To School Today...
My Mom's In Prison And I Don't Have A Ride."

ORDER FORM

Name _____

Address _____

_____

Telephone _____

Please Send Me:

_____ Copies of **"I Can't Come To School Today...
My Mom's In Prison And I Don't Have A Ride."**

_____ **Total @ $13.95 per copy**

_____ California Residents please add **7.25%** sales tax
(**$1.01** per book)

_____ Add **$2.00** per book for postage & handling

_____ **Total Enclosed**

☐ Please send me information about Positive
Behavioral Intervention trainings.

☐ Please send me information about Language Arts
Workshops.

When ordering, make checks payable to **Quiet Thunder
Publishing**. For book orders from outside of the U.S. please
send *only* checks drawn on a U.S. bank in U.S. dollars, or an
international postal money order in U.S. dollars. Please allow
4-6 weeks for delivery.

Send orders to:
Quiet Thunder Publishing
P.O. Box 2097-A
Ventura, CA 93002

"I Can't Come To School Today...
My Mom's In Prison And I Don't Have A Ride."

ORDER FORM

Name_____

Address_____

_____

Telephone_____

Please Send Me:

_____   Copies of **"I Can't Come To School Today...
           My Mom's In Prison And I Don't Have A Ride."**

_____   **Total @ $13.95 per copy**

_____   California Residents please add **7.25%** sales tax
                             (**$1.01** per book)

_____   Add **$2.00** per book for postage & handling

_____   **Total Enclosed**

☐   Please send me information about Positive
      Behavioral Intervention trainings.

☐   Please send me information about Language Arts
      Workshops.

When ordering, make checks payable to **Quiet Thunder
Publishing**. For book orders from outside of the U.S. please
send only checks drawn on a U.S. bank in U.S. dollars, or an
international postal money order in U.S. dollars. Please allow
4-6 weeks for delivery.

Send orders to:
Quiet Thunder Publishing
P.O. Box 2097-A
Ventura, CA 93002